insideout

p o e m s

l. l. barkat

IAM

International Arts Movement
New York, NY

International Arts Movement
38 West 39th Street, 3rd Floor
New York, NY 10018

© 2009, 2nd edition 2014 by L.L. Barkat

Poems in memory of Flight 447 are fictionalized and not meant to
represent any actual persons. Likewise, the poem about Sudan
does not reflect on a specific ethnic or political group. The poem
"Incident" is based on a story told by Dava Sobel in *The Planets*
(Viking Adult, 2005). The poem "Return to Sloansville" includes a
reference to Budweiser, a trademark of Anheuser-Busch.

Cover image by Gail Nadeau.
www.firlefanzgallery.com/Nadeau.html

Illustrations by Sara Barkat.

ISBN 978-0-9843501-0-0

Library of Congress Cataloging-in-Publication Data:
Barkat, L.L.
        [Poems.]
        Insideout: poems/L.L. Barkat
        Includes index
        ISBN 978-0-9843501-0-0
        Library of Congress Control Number: 2009912777

To my mother,
who gave us poetry

CONTENTS

Why

When I was small, my mother often tucked me beside her on the nubby gold couch, classic book in hand, and brought me to tears with narrative poems about everything from an African chief sold into slavery, to a vain young—and, as it turned out, underdressed—woman who died of frostbite on her way to a party.

How I loved a good poem, and I wasn't shy about requesting favorite after favorite. Some of these poems worked themselves into memory, giving me a longlasting poetic sense that made me a confident reader of poems.

Still, for many years I believed that writing poetry was something other people did. I don't recall trying to craft a single poem before college, at which point it was confirmed—I was not, nor would ever be, a writer of poems. Assigned to write a sonnet, I produced something so dismal that all I remember of it today is just that: my sonnet was a failure. I would have to leave the creation of verse to such as Keats and Hopkins.

This is the tale of poetry-writing for many people. Unable to copy the clipped meter of Dickinson or the narrative voice of Frost, they give up and leave the effort to others. If the writing of poetry were not such a satisfying and healing endeavor, this would be a fine conclusion. It is not, however, a conclusion I encourage.

Few of us who play with words will become the next poet laureate, but why should this stop us? If we can read poetry well, or speak poetry in normal conversation (which many of us uncannily do), then it might not hurt to try writing poetry too. At some point I must have decided this for myself. For better or for worse, you hold that decision in your hands.

L.L. Barkat, 2009

Looking back at *InsideOut*, my first collection of poems, I marvel at what has happened over the course of five years. For one, I have learned a few things about line breaks and so have felt compelled to come back and make some necessary changes. I promise I won't return again.

For another, I've since written seemingly more complex poems: sestinas (one published at *The Best American Poetry*), sonnets, and ghazals. They have their appeal.

But I am pleased with these old poems—many of them deceptively simple like haiku—and happy with how they have stood up over time, at least for me. Sometimes we look back on our writing and feel it does not capture what we'd want it to capture anymore. Not so with these words.

Maybe it is the timelessness of Nature that infuses them, or maybe the poems somehow illuminate parts of me that are deep and enduring, though some of my circumstances have changed. I'll keep the poems. And I hope, after all, they will keep you—through many seasons.

L.L. Barkat, 2014

FALL

I committed to sit outdoors every day, for at least the time it would take to finish a cup of tea. It was nothing fancy, mind you; each day for a year, I sat in my back yard under a pine tree. Having begun the endeavor in winter, Fall was my final season. I used to think the time of leaves drifting, air crisping, apples ripening was my favorite. Now I am undecided...

Autumn Milkweed

A thousand seeds
burst
from this rough belly,
fling themselves
to the wind...
a tumble
of silken forgetfulness.

Almonds

I remember the scent
and how you crushed them;
brown skins
turned to dust,
scattered like spilled cinnamon.

Visit

The first time
I entered
this living room,
it was
a dying room.

Evan, propped
on the narrow
blue couch, the life
nearly pressed out
of him, turned

to me and smiled,
lifted a tremored
hand to touch
my warmth, my
life. I did not

know I would
buy this house
a mere year later,
nor that I would
sit under the pine

he planted out back,
rescued
from up the street
when the bulldozing
began. I did not

know what it meant
that moment, my hand
touching his,
in this living dying
room, with its

hearth, old
ashes, glass doors
closed against the day.

The Turning

Sky brimming blue
barely held back, ready
to spill, overrun hills
burning orange
with desire.
Fall coming on.

Prayer

I am
two folded wings,
waiting
for a stirring of air.

Stayed

for Ann Voskamp

Why do we not
leave home.
Is it really for fear
of what lies
beyond, or rather
for fear
that the roof
will abscond
with the doors
and the shutters
we've always known.
And who would they blame
if it happened
just so, if the whole
curtained place
simply picked up its stakes,
disappeared on the wind
in our absence. What
are we really afraid of,
why do we not
leave home.

Grace

On the back porch,
it molders green,
licks
slow bites
swallows the base
of a terra cotta
pot.

Priest

How I fear
facing them,
empty pleats,
Zechariah mute.

Mischief pine
has decked the little
bush beside me
with bronze needle
tinsel, draped her
in surprise holiday.

Moon shimmers, glassy blue
night. I lie under glistening
pine, watch house lights shine
over empty white yard while my
girl cuts cucumber crescents
on grain-gold kitchen counters.

Maple

Afire 'neath
sun's last flames—
phoenix upon its nest.

Maple II

Fine in yellow
dress, readies herself
for winter's dance.

Golden
grasses fallen—
straw reaching
sideways to
escape destiny.

Kale is
purpling,
bluing and
purpling.

Little lemon tongues,
wagged off at last.

Dogwood
wears the finest
lace, woven from
day's departure.

Fall's dry fingers open
winter's white duvet,
shake and ready it.

"Tip, tip, tip," says the rain
to my sorrow. "Trust me, do."
And the hemlocks in their stillness
say much the same.

Scent
of death upon
the leaves;
how lovely
the fragrance.

Fall sneaks into
the house, hiding on
my skin and hair.

Trees black, struck against
faded cobalt sky and the sun
leaking tears, yellow, pink.

Red berries on
thorn bush— bright
packages for birds.

Lone forsythia bud
spills October's secret:
too flirtatious with the sun!

Geese call overhead,
fading sound of
goodbye summer.

Yellow and red
splash against
my black umbrella.

Lightning flashes
and I write
of yellow leaves.

I shall not
miss
the mosquitoes!

I have heard
they harvest wild rice
by hand,
bending stems
that rise from waters,
knocking them
for chocolate
seed.

Cataclysmic

It began as a regular day,
yet at 2:59 eastern time,

the universe flipped upside
down. Andromeda slid into

Sol. I lost sense of gravity,
matter. Ate stars. By the fistful.

Holy Writ

I spied God
meddling with
my keyboard,
skipping from
a to z like He
was some kind
of Alpha and
Omega who
could ply
a whole world,
ex nihilo, presto,
from the chaos.

Lingua

Words ply themselves
into circles, springs,
say shocking things
when I let them
fly from purple pens,
flee the margins.

Foyer

Who looks
at the new straw
hat, remembering
Grandma,

how she beat
brazen rays each
day by sneaking
under a brim

like that. And who
notices the wrought
iron roses now
hung askew

on our cherry
coat rack; she
wrung pits
out of red fruit

too, swatted flies,
rolled tart sweet
flesh, juice into
crust, but that is

another story;
I am asking you
about the roses,
broken, and a

missing screw,
but you are busy
arranging tailored
black wool

on a cool hook worn
brass blue; we're
just in the hall
after all, we're just

passing through.

Evening Prayer

Alone tonight, beside
an open window,
I hear trees moving,
whispering to wind.

Would that in my dark
places, I could lean in,
let you tender move and
make me whisper too.

Spied

My soul was in
the oven, five days
old, almost empty but
for a few crusty flakes
and stray apples spilling
over the side of a glass
pie plate, threatening stainless
steel racks and self-cleaning
walls with caramelized sugar.

Offering

I am just
a simple cup
on counter
bare scrubbed
scoured of day's
too sour lemonade,
catsup fingerprints
hints of cream
loss of dreams
in coffee sipped,
dripped past
crumbs 'til day
is numb with
stars. Pick me
up, sweep into
me the dregs
of play. That's
what I'm for
when empty
anyway.

Gift

Boxed taped paper
flapped folded fitted
sealed kissed sent felt
burst open
let me
be.

The Picking

Who knew the apple
would turn

blue. It was just
blushing towards

red when I said to
myself,

ah this is for you,
my angel.

Teacup

I remember traveling
in his suitcase, white athletic
sock stuffed in my belly to keep
me from breaking, rocking 'midst
clouds, and your hand's first
touch bringing me to birth
on that wooden table,
and your lips.

Verse

What is poetry,
she asked,
fetching it to me
with full hands.
How could I
answer the woman?
I do not know
what it is
any more
than she. I guess it must be
marks on tender
skin, bearers of sin,
cool cups of rain
and bottles of tears
collected on midnight
trains from the eyes
of old men, old women
and infants traveling
to God knows where,
it hangs and is lifted
from our hair
goes onward and
onward speaking itself,
tripping us
as we debark
chewing-gum-mottled
metal stairs.

Song

I found my soul
in an attic
circa 1932,
toes naked
near a scruffy yellow
Teletubbie,
fingers
spreading ivory
pages, Whitman
clothed in 40's
faded burlap,
once green
like the grass.
Soul voice,
undisguised,
was whisper
whispering,
gently turning
over under rafters,
urge and urge
and urging
a sweet clear
song of myself.

Couch

If we had known,
considered,
when we slapped down
a few hundred dollars
for dark green paisley
with a hidden
sleeper, if we had seen
it coming,
the shredded chintz,
tatters, depressions
and how we would not
care to repair it
because it's too short
for my spouse to sit on
(hurts his back,
he says), then maybe
we would have dug
a little deeper, sacrificed more
to save for something
lasting, to keep through a lifetime
and pass on to children,

grandchildren. As it goes
we need to toss birthdays
stray tortilla crumbs
sweat of bodies
embraced, stolen kisses
accidental spray of suckling
milk, toddler bounces
and goodbyes to daddy
at the window. If we'd but known.

Out

I found you
tucked between
black pinstripe
and woolen

plaid. One strap
already slipped
from a white
plastic hanger

as if you knew
I would reach
through any minute
now, shake red

silk free of darkness,
slide you over
my shoulders, let your
sweet cherry bow rest

beneath my breast.
I remember now, you
used to belong to
petite Asian friend

of sister. Did she
have a baby doll face
and what was the cut
of her hair? What would

she think if she saw
you now, making
silver-headed church women
whisper and stare?

Manners

Nice
is what I play
when I pretend
that red is pink,
when I care what
people think.

Trekking

I walked the world,
feet wet with bright dew
of morning's breath

in dappled woods I came
upon birches slender slight
asway and early set

with fall buds, tight and hard
inviting the passerby's
tongue and suck

what luck that I found
them, on the way.

WINTER

January is a harsh month in the Northeast. It sends people indoors to the solace of hearth and hot chocolate. It is not a month of beginnings, but it became one for me. I got it into my head to sit outdoors for a brief while, every day for a year. It's not my fault this notion was born in the dead of winter. The first day and many that ensued were below-zero. The snow was deep that year. In the end, winter surprised me...

Forsake me not,
despite the news
the gods
the mantras preaching,
wait.

Sister

upon the arrival of Summer Rain

You
birthed
life,
barely
suckling,
broken
hearted,
tenacious
beyond
imagining.

January

Air bites presses
cold cajoles
rushes sears dares
the little garland tree
stripped against
an ever-darkening
night. Stars twinkle
blue cool far
bare promises.
Impossible white
tips evergreens
blankets dead
leaves, eases to
depressions of
animal feet—
squirrel rabbit
racoon deer.
Bamboo dry rustles
casts shadows long.
No song of light
seems probable
around these winter
corners, streets laid
with ice.

Apology

for Maria and Jarit

I swear I was on my way
to see you, there in your igloo
it took five men and a whole day
to build. You were drying

polar bear meat, melting
months-old snow to pour into
my tin cup. The day was white
on white, and I was swerving snow

dunes on a black and yellow
skidoo, picking up meteorites
along the way (where they
came from, I can't say).

I had a pound of precious rice
in my pocket—a rare treat
in an Antarctica kitchen—and a thousand
kisses for you on my lips.

I swear I was on my way.

*

Do not think
I am pliant as the water
'neath day's descending
cherry sun.

Bend me too far,
my sweet, and I
snap
bright with sorrow.

Senility

for my aunt, mother and Grammy

I remember
when I existed
in more than just
a scrap of your mind...
you knew my name,
the contour of my face,
my petals and my thorns,
in wild, blushing color.

That was before
the outlines
of forgetfulness
began encroaching,
to steal away
the me I was
in you.

Senility II

for my father, Joan and Grandma

What golden fountain
do you sip from, Mother,
and what angels see
as you waltz in sleepy dreams
obscured, eclipsed
from a trembling me.

In Your Dream

i.

I was the wind
that knocked at the glass, that tipped
the candle that burned the kitchen;
all that remained was a golden fork.

ii.

I was the sound
of shattering, of gold
chattering amidst the wild
wild flames.

iii.

I was the fork
golden and shining,
pricking the crumbs
scattered across
white linens of
your dream.

iv.

I was the story
in the burning book,
leading you beyond
frost and fields
lapped by time
towards a clearing.

v.

I was the curtain
that brushed your face
promised to shield you
from day's
too-bright arrival.

iv.

I was the flame
that laughed
at goodbye.

In Memory of Flight 447 En Route from
Brazil to France

Wreckage, 447

They found an airplane
seat, fuel slick, orange life
vest, pieces of white debris
bobbing in salty water. But
did anyone see the strand
of amber hair she'd left
on his lapel, cherry lipstick
smudge, and the place
where teeth met flesh.

Black Box, 447

What indestructible secrets
does the black box hold. Besides electrical
failure, did it record his intention
to return her key for good on Monday,

does it hold her regret for being
too easy that night they cut the deal
on the purchase of rubber
for ten factories in the South. Will it tell

how the child lay dreaming
of chocolate gateaux with cherries
and how his mother had just
dabbed whipped cream

on his freckled nose to make him laugh.
Or can it say how—while the boy
was still unwrapping presents,
'midst screams he thought were party

sounds—the woman took him in her
arms one last time, as if for the first
time, and pressed his face against
milk-white silk and breaking breast.

Assumption, 447

A religious man,
he had always hoped
to be taken up
like Elijah—chariots on
the clouds, lightning flashing
his soul to God. And so it was
he got his wish, white
light streaking, hurling mortal
shell. Still it puzzled him
as to why the sky opened up
below, rather than sucking
him heavenward.

Song of Sudan

You travel past equator 'til
the sand whips over day
and night descends quite still.

Cloth veils the face of women ill
and well (you cannot say);
you travel past equator 'til

the Nile snakes its shrill
regret of war, while battle is at bay
and night descends quite still.

By morning, sun begins to stalk and fill
the cracks of every hiding place
you travel past equator 'til

deep griefs unravel will
to rebuild shattered clay
and night descends quite still.

An ibis eyes you, dips her beak to kill
some silver flash like bullet play
you travel past equator 'til
the night descends quite still.

Snow sifts
softly, oh
so gently
covers
me.

Christmas

wind whips
flakes fleck
dark pine

leans shivers
shakes cold
grace pours

sky opens
soul bends
breaks.

*

Blue pearls
smashed
like glass.

Snow descends in dancing sheets
sparkling cloth, flung out
by a dressmaker's hands.

Red thorn berry
shriveled, deepened
to muted cranberry—
too-long suckled
by winter's
urge.

Snow empties the sky
to a bare whiteness
but it fills me, fills me.

Hemlocks sway, twigs
snap, slap the air—bold
tango at yard's edge.

Blueberry bushes
stripped lean, amber
crimson against
a bronze needle bed.

I did not
want
to leave the warmth
of the kitchen,
scent
of fresh-roasted granola
and evening's
potato curry.

Disappearance

It is not just
your voice
that one day

evaporated

poof! a black hole
where once
there were stars.

It is, too, a comet's
tail of words
that sang to you,

now muted

at the far edge
of space and
time.

Instructions

for Patricia Cook

What to do when a best friend's husband dies
on the eve of your little girl's birthday:

Hang up the phone, lean into your counter
in a kind of conscious faint. Moan.
Moan, a deep cry that comes from a place
you didn't know existed, tremble
feel the ice sensation that begins
rising and falling within you
like Northern Lights
shimmering up and down
a midnight sky.

Take out the black-handled
Henckels and a yellow onion,
chop pearly flesh into perfect
little squares. Mince summer
garlic. Scrape all into a cast iron
pan. Add dried oregano, because you can't
think about harvesting right now... fresh
oregano just outside the kitchen door.

Turn to the sink, begin. One glass,
one dish at a time. Watch suds play
at edges of cobalt blue, fall onto

stainless steel, slide down the drain. Moan
again. A labored moan rising to a muted wail
(you dare not wake the children).

Curse the maker
of lawn mowers. Beg the man
to come back and this time decide
upon a nap instead of simple exercise
of back and forth on green, where he has
fallen. Did fall. Ask God to turn back time,
if only for this one whose heart has failed
him. Let it not be so, that he has
fallen.

Turn off the pewter faucet,
blue flame. Put wilted onions
and herbs in the bottom of a crock pot,
where they will have to wait until tomorrow.
Flick off recessed lighting.
Go up red oak stairs. Sleep,
a dreamless sleep.

In the morning, sing happy birthday
to your eight-year-old. Kiss her
on the cheek and forehead. Hold her to your

chest. Give her the black-handled scissors
so she may go out into the green.

The birthday sauce will be needing basil, fresh.

And she will go out skipping,
snip it for you at the tender neck.
Put it in your hand with soft, round
fingers. Toss her head and smile.

Acceptance

has come slow
the way my grass
flows smooth, long
winter-expectant
in the front yard
dark green and thick
dotted with fragile
golden leaves
I've not wanted
to rake away.

Ignition

Who can say when sorrow
will glide into the heart
like some Trojan Horse
on wheels.

Today
beneath a bronzing maple,
it rode in on the curl
of a lemon-blushed leaf.

Aqua windshield,
still content to mirror clouds
waltzing in an opal sky,
provided no resistance.

Laundry Day

Women gather
chatter find
wading places
dip jeans workshirts
onesies bibs
in bubbling stream
wash away milk
blood semen.
I slap cotton
wool linen 'gainst
rounded rocks.
No one sees
the pearl button
crack, ricochet
float away.

Laundry Day II

No one
hears cry of weave,
memories stinging
singing stubbornly
clinging, swearing
they'll hold on
through final
hangings.

You

move me
with
your sorrow, I
open my mouth
and it is like
the promise of apples,
honey fragrant
on air,
a barely there
wish. I swallow
emptiness.

Nostalgia

I miss
the place
that cradled stars
in blackness,
even while
my heart
searched for
the elusive
lullaby.

Hibernate.

It is not
a killing word,
a crisis

word
a trauma word.
It is

a tender deep
warm primal
lay me

down to sleep
word, a nestle
into rest

word that
touches darkness,
unafraid.

SPRING

In the semi-urban environment where I make my home, it is hard to embrace solitude for even fifteen minutes. The culture of the place agitates and urges. No time for rain (it will muss up your hair for the next appointment), no time to watch Spring's first blossoms. Seasons turn and we miss the nuances. But I had committed to sitting still in my yard and watching. So I saw things I never saw before...

Shall I teach
you the way
of a blossom,
the way of a cherry
twisting beneath
her stem,
shall I.

I was the moonlight
ringed by heaven,
sent by fairies
to make you,
if possible,
once again believe.

Rain
smears my face
iris tremble-ache.

Quintessential love,
two peas in a sweet
curved pod.

Return to Sloansville

I close my eyes,
blot out one hundred
and fifty shale driveways
pickup trucks, Ford
pintos, trailers barely
tied to this ground
by wires, gas lines
cable TV.

I can still see
dirt road, Queen
Anne's Lace, goldenrod
blue chicory,
field mice nesting
under leaning timothy
and the apple orchard
rooted beyond tall firs

where a woman
in navy sweat pants
and red Budweiser t-shirt
is just now hanging laundry
to drift upon the wind,
sing with ghosts
of spring white
blossoms, honeybees.

Yet

I remember
our walks
when I was
a child.

On no-moon
nights,
there were
yet
stars.

The Watching

If memories were sparrows,
mine would gather behind
a house half finished aluminum

sided against the landscape, windows
glazed from the inside out with smoke
of cigarette and venison burning.

They would crowd in lavender lilac,
above the intersection where each year
a robin laid impossible blue eggs,

one of which it seems would always
break, sully the perfect roundness
of a mother's mud-patched efforts

to prevent a deadly cracking. Sparrow
memories would rock limbs, tremble
leaves, blot out the threat of rain

while brown-haired girls peered over
rim of tight worked straw to watch
a miracle of twin eggs coming to birth.

Journey

by Sara Barkat, age 12

The sails unfurl
the cries ring in the air,
the ship is on the waves of curls.

Ship rides o'er seas of pearl
while dragon rests in lair,
the sails unfurl.

Setting off to lands of kings and earls
the sailors eat some pears,
the ship is on the waves of curls.

One seaman's known to love a girl
one boy climbs up a mount, on dare,
the sails unfurl.

Some on the ship have seen Arur
a family has a small pet bear,
the sails unfurl
the ship is on the waves of curls.

King

by Sonia Barkat, age 9

A ring? Just
sing for me the
king. All that
nonsense about
gifts. Just sing for me
the king. A royal carriage
to an airport... deluxe
vacation; I have to
run my kingdom.
Just sing for me
the king.

Forsythia, triple
leafed fleur de lis
gracing the woods.

How desperately
the dog next door
tells the world
that I am
here.

Hemlocks whisper,
"Hush, hush, hush,
the girl can hear us."

Furled leaves of wild
garlic mustard and, soon,
forsythia breakfasts!

Spring's
first butterfly—
pale yellow flutter
on the wind!

Three cardinals volley
chirps, swing calls—
bush to hemlock to pine.

Mate

Cardinal calls shrill
in his baudy red
tights and g-string,

won't sit still, shut
down, give peace
to the woods till he finds

her, kisses and blinds
her, rush of feathers
trill, thrill, ebullient spill.

Hemlock branches
bounce like babies
in their swings.

Miniature
face of the baby
cardinal, tiny
promise of
crest-to-be
above his eyes
like a hat.

Look around! Watch
the hemlocks swinging,
hear the 'thtick thtick' of
little pinecones dropping,
touch the pearl-blue sky,
see the buds swelling.

New squirrel
in the woods,
black like a
velvet cat.

The air is silk,
morning raises yet again
its veil of longing.

Do not say
there is too little time
to lay upon
my lap. Let me riffle
your brown curls,
court the curve
of your chin and cheek.

Curry leaf
floats, curls
'midst black onion
seeds, brown sauce,
and I taste
your love.

Cherry rose,
oblivion
once bared.

In Lieu of the
New York Times

If words were
clovers,
I'd pluck mine
and lay them
at your doorstep,
retreat to shade
of oak,
watch you become
a child again,
poke past purple
spikes, nip tender
white tips
with teeth, freely sip
raw sugar, lick
your lip.

Porch

Come rest
a while in the red
rocker, tell your
cares to me. Day
is still young, wisteria
hangs purple from
the wainscot porch roof,
dew poised on its turning
leaf. Drink a shivering
glass of sweet tea, suck
lemon on your way
to settled sugar endings.
Rock your cares
into my floorboards. Come,
rest a while with me.

The Wait

You aren't
the only one
waiting
for tongue
and cheek,
wishing
to fall asleep,
to hold
perchance
to dream.

Bottled

I am fizzle
fazzle pizazz
snap crackle,
slide your hand
past my red belt
take me by the
ribbed neck
set teeth on edge
flick fluted tin
and, pop!

Ruby moon,
May apples
and you beneath
this galaxy, peering
light at me.

SUMMER

*During summer, I often went out at night; day was too
brilliant, too warm. If you have spent any time out of doors
when it is dark, you will remember how deep are the fragrances
and how enchanting. They speak of love, intensity, consum-
mation—echoing the colorful fruits of day...peach, plum,
currant, strawberry...*

Incident

Dava Sobel
envied her friend,
who had somehow
got hold of moon dust—
about a tablespoon
or so, from an astro lover boy.

It could have been bottled
for posterity, sprinkled
in the garden or put in biscuits
to feed the five thousand,
if only
the woman had not
swallowed the whole
damn dose of it.

I kid you not, she claimed
it for her own and now
she is one with the moon.

Moon's full-orbed
body glows through
chintz of cloud.

Jasmine would not
crackle; it is too soft for that.
Whisper it might, a sweet song of
goodnight.

Moss relents
and so the day, I break
beneath the shaded tree,
the promise of your fingers
falling softly.

Your bangles
whispered glass love
through marble halls, your hair
coconut fragrant, hands
henna red.

Summer

I love
when the
white lily comes,
iridescent urn
turned to the sun.

Ambrosia

I swallow
history, future,
all the flowers
ever bloomed,
flutter my eyelashes
now saffron pollen
freckled, undone.

Surely the currant,
with its sour bite,
did not tempt thee, Eve,
unless the serpent
had upon his person
a small spoon of sugar.

Frilly skirted
chanterelle, how you
beckon, fling.

Fourth of July

Would that the night
could preserve this
sight of stars
and stripes, red green
fuschia blue and spirals too
like Goldilock's
curls all strung with fire.

Works

Bang! Shots in the dark
expire in less than
a beat of forever.

Storm During Fireworks

Up go rockets, burst!
Sizzle, sizzle, consummation
in the clouds. Rain has come.

After Fireworks

I gather my girls under black
umbrella. Two sparklers at my
side, I slip into the night.

I, Alfred

Do I
dare...
to eat
a peach?

Muse

You are not the blonde
beauty I'd been taught
to believe in, Renaissance-buxom,
fawning over my every word

and feeding me grapes
while I sop up inspiration from
the sweat of your pores. I wish you'd
stop yawning, picking your teeth

and flicking stray peach skins
over my notes. Who can work
in the presence of such disdain,
who can stay sane, pen the next

masterpiece while your eyes
look so vexed. You are not
the helpmeet I ordered, not the glass
of red wine nor the rich, fine

chocolate they promised in sonnets.
I bet money you like it this way, wielding
a tray of miniature mincemeat pies,
not lifting a finger to help me swat flies.

Page 5

The menu
says strawberry
shortcake

with whipped cream

but here's the deal:
I remember what's real,
my mother's child-small

hands turning flour

sugar, shortening
the "size of a big egg"
so the old recipe

instructed. I remember

sun-kissed fields
of furrows, hills my
grandmother's rough

patched yet painted

hands turned and raised
to grow strawberries blushed
and bleeding real juice,

not perfumed water

that pretends ripeness
cut and strewn over too-
sweet cake. I remember

cream, real, whipped.

Harvest

Three little
blueberries
I will hide
inside to ripen.

Jasmine, orange,
plum. The bowl tips,
I stain my fingers with
nectar-scented love.

Trees
wrestle
the air.

Squirrel tail
wiggles, a weightless
question mark.

Light plays
upon the pine,
dips her in golden oil.

Puffs of pine needles
shimmy like fat grass
hula skirts.

Let the mosquito
land. Then you can
swat him.

Hemlocks
bow in turn,
do obeisance
to the house.

Squirrel
purrs,
soft-trills.

Trees embrace
midnight,
drink starshine
as if from burning
bowls.

Silken web undulates,
a lady's private wash
upon the wind.

Pine branches...
spokes in two directions,
lateral 'round trunk
and spinning 'cross knobbly
joints of each protusion—
wheels within wheels,
Ezekiel tree.

Wild cowboy squirrels
buck through hemlocks;
cardinals shoot out, cry.

Spider
spun
while I
rested,
did not
know.

When Morning Comes

I open my mouth and breathe the day,
wish for a kiss like the one this golden
trumpet of jewelweed is getting full
on the mouth. Furry bumblebee embraces

her like there's no tomorrow. And I remember
to hold the moment because it's true, there may not
be a morning after. And this is why I pause when
rusty shovel unearths rotted pit, peach long gone,

her hope for progeny emptied but home to red
ants now, tiny thousands pouring forth like honey,
spilling onto cocoa shells newly lain beneath
the hyssop, soft pink and pungent. Now I trouble

the bronze-suited honeybee who is fumbling Russian
Sage, tickling her purply-blue tongues, riding her
shining silver leaves that curl in rainbowed mist.
Shall I forget the three-leafed maple fragment red

upon the stair, its green seeds like outstretched arms
now blushing dusty rose. Let me not forget these
seeds, nor the catbird who delights to echo each
whine of my clipping shears, nor the Bible Leaf

relieved of yellow flower but fragrant still when I
break a spear and press it to my face. Let me not
forget the white carnation, purple aster, and the stars
who shut their eyes and sleep when morning comes.

Cleopatra's Summer

Forgive me, Mark,
your ship arrived
my almond eyes
could never let
you go.

Imagine
the scent, your skirt
burning like flowered stars.

Love

I
became
lines
without
end.

If sunflowers
touched us lightly
as pollen on a
blue day, would we not
care again, dream.

Homecoming

for my niece, Summer Rain

From birth, long months
you had lain triple broken
hearted, needle pricked,
wired, ravaged by fire

of fever and untold pain. Still.
Just yesterday you quietly came,
a blue cloud of promise o'er rise
of hill—late summer rain.

Index

Also Available

L.L. Barkat lived a kind of natural poetry amidst woods and streams of her growing-up place. This poetry infuses her other titles, like *Rumors of Water*, *The Novelist*, and *Love, Etc.*

"a great eye for details and a luminous style"

Byron Borger, Hearts and Minds Books

"Delicate, suggestive, clever"

Carl Sharpe, editor at Versewrights

"reminiscent of the prose of Annie Dillard"

Monica Tenney, Congregational Libraries Today

"To state the pleasurable, Barkat is a damn fine writer"

Hubert O'Hearn, former editor Herald de Paris, *Contributing Editor* San Francisco Book Review

About International Arts Movement

International Arts Movement is a non-profit arts organization that gathers artists and creative catalysts to wrestle with the deep questions of art and humanity. Through lectures, performances, exhibitions, screenings, projects and workshops, IAM equips artists of all disciplines to generate good, true and beautiful cultural artifacts: sign-posts pointing toward the "world that ought to be."

A portion of the proceeds from this book benefits International Arts Movement.

www.internationalartsmovement.org